25 Spanish Plays for Emergent Readers

BY CAROL PUGLIANO-MARTIN

SCHOLASTIC
PROFESSIONAL BOOKS

NEW YORK • TORONTO • LONDON • AUCKLAND • SYDNEY
MEXICO CITY • NEW DELHI • HONG KONG

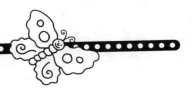

To Scott,

who is

"just-right"

for me.

Cover design by Jaime Lucero
Cover illustration by Larry Daste
Interior play illustrations by Ellen Joy Sasaki; activity illustrations by James Graham Hale
Interior design by Kathy Massaro

ISBN: 0-439-10546-3
Copyright © 1998 by Carol Pugliano-Martin
All rights reserved.
Printed in the U.S.A.

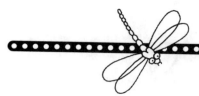

Contents

Celebrate the Seasons

Exploring Nature

All About Animals

Plays for Anytime

Introduction

I recently spoke to a primary school teacher who told me that many of his students enjoy reading stories aloud. So he began to adapt stories into plays by creating scenes with speaking parts for his students to play. I thought that his task, while very admirable, seemed like a lot of work for a busy teacher. And that is how this book came about. This collection of original plays is specially tailored for emergent readers. All you need is a copy machine and some eager children!

These plays do not require building sets, making costumes, or putting on productions. Instead, they offer an easy and inviting way to use the form of plays as a tool for helping young children enter the exciting world of reading.

There are 25 reproducible plays in this book, based on favorite primary themes that children adore, such as seasonal celebrations, animals, and the natural world. Some of the features and benefits of using these plays follow.

❀ Each play is easy to read, using words from leveled word lists. Some plays use simple and fun made-up words that will help children discover the playfulness of language.

❀ The plays use devices such as rhyme, repetitive language, and predictability to help young children gain confidence as readers and take pleasure from the experience of reading. Appealing illustrations are an aid to comprehension.

❀ Sentences are short for easy reading and most do not run beyond one line. Type size is large for emergent-reader eyes.

❀ The number of speaking parts in each play ranges from two to enough parts for the whole class. Many plays can be adjusted to use fewer or more speakers as you see fit. You may also wish to have students team up to read the same part together.

❀ Many plays are based on real-life situations, which helps children to connect reading to their daily lives.

❀ Reading these plays aloud provides a less competitive, less stressful environment for emergent readers. Plus, research has shown that reading aloud helps oral language development, an important element in emergent reading.

❀ In addition to the plays, there is a simple-to-do extension activity for each play (see pages 6 to 14) that will help you to integrate your students' play-reading experiences across the curriculum.

You may find these tips helpful as you use this book with your class:

BEFORE READING THE PLAYS

❀ Photocopy the play and distribute a copy to each student. Also, write the play on chart paper, so you can point along as children read aloud.

❀ Divide speaking parts into smaller or larger groupings as desired. For example, three children might read the same part.

❀ After assigning parts, hand out crayons or markers so that children can highlight their lines. This will make it easier for children to identify their own parts as they read.

❀ Read the play aloud to your class before they read it on their own. This will help to familiarize children with the play's content and action. Go over vocabulary that might be new to students.

WHILE READING THE PLAYS

❀ Incorporate phonics lessons into play readings. For example, you might challenge children to find all of the words in a play that begin with /b/.

❀ Ask children to identify rhyming language or repeated refrains.

❀ Divide the class into reading groups to read different plays together. Each group can work independently and then come together as a class to share their reading.

❀ Invite children to act out the plays using simple paper-bag or stick puppets to portray different characters. Using a puppet behind a simple stage will help to create a feeling of safety and anonymity for children who may feel uncomfortable performing in front of a group. (You can make an instant stage by covering a table with a floor-length tablecloth and having children crouch behind it.) Give children the option to read from their scripts while performing, or to memorize their lines, if they prefer.

AFTER READING THE PLAYS

❀ To assess comprehension of the plays, ask follow-up questions after reading.

❀ Encourage children to write their own plays. One way to start is by inviting students to write "What Happened Next?" episodes that continue the plays.

❀ Have children take home copies of the plays to read with family members.

❀ Put on simple productions of the plays as presentations on Visitors' Day.

I hope you and your students will discover the joy of words, reading, and drama through the plays in this book!

Carol Pugliano-Martin

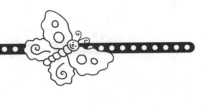

Curriculum Connections

CELEBRATE THE SEASONS

Time for Fall

ALL FALL DOWN

Invite students to stand up and pretend they are leaves about to fall off a tree in autumn. Have them talk about how they feel. Then, invite students to pretend they are slowly falling to the ground. They can make noises if they wish. What kind of sounds might a falling leaf make? Later, ask students how they felt to be falling leaves. Did they feel like the leaves in the play? Have they ever been afraid of trying something new, only to discover that the experience was fun? Ask students to share their experiences.

Autumn Sounds

GUESS THAT SOUND

Play a "Guess That Sound" game with your class. Invite children to pick a sound that they would like to try to simulate. They can choose crunching leaf sounds from the play or pick any other sound. Provide materials and containers for the children to make their sounds. (boxes, tissue paper, brushes, combs, pennies) For example, place dried beans or rice in a covered shoe box. When shaken, it makes a good rain sound. As one child shares his or her sound, have the rest of the class, with eyes closed, guess what sound the child has simulated. Then, challenge students to guess what the child is using to make that sound.

Snowflakes

COOPERATIVE SNOWFLAKES

Invite children to make their own sparkly snowflakes. Use a paper plate or large round lid to trace several circles on old file folders. Cut them out to make circle templates. Have students trace and cut out circles from light-colored construction paper. Next, let students brush on "ice crystals"

(a mixture of 3 tablespoons salt and 1/4 cup warm water). Let the papers dry overnight. The following day, have students fold and cut their circles as shown to make snowflakes.

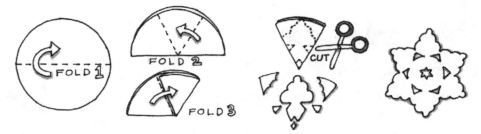

Chances are, most of the children's snowflakes will look different from one another's. Use this opportunity to relate their snowflakes to those in the play. Do any look like flowers? Do any look like stars? Later, place all of the snowflakes on a bulletin board in a snowman shape to illustrate the point of the play: even though all of the snowflakes look different, when they are put together, they can make a snowman. Begin a discussion on how this concept can apply to the class as a whole. How can children in the class, like the snowflakes, cooperate to achieve the same goals?

Groundhog Day

SPREAD THE NEWS

Celebrate Groundhog Day by reading or performing this play, using whichever ending applies. Then make a mock television newscast of the outcome. Invite students to play the newscaster, reporters on the scene, people being interviewed about the event, and the groundhog. Begin by having the newscaster tell television viewers what happened when the groundhog came out of its burrow. Then have the reporter interview the groundhog by asking, "How do you feel after [seeing/not seeing] your shadow today?" Next, have another reporter interview people about what they think about an early spring or six more weeks of winter. End with the newscaster wrapping up the story in the "TV studio."

Hooray for Spring!

SPRINGTIME POETRY

What are some signs of spring where you live? Ask students to name some of their favorite things relating to this season. Then write their responses on the board. Using all of the class suggestions, write a poem together about their favorite spring things. Copy the poem onto a large piece of chart paper and display it on a bulletin board. Invite children to draw or paint pictures to accompany the poem. Read the poem aloud together on the first day of spring to celebrate its arrival!

EXPLORING NATURE

From Seed to Plant

GROW, SEED, GROW

Help children construct "see-inside" growing containers to get a close-up look at a seed's underground growth. Cut two slits in a paper cup as shown. Fold down the cut panel, and tape plastic wrap over this opening. Then fold the cut panel back up again. Place a rubber band around the cup to hold the panel in place. Use a pencil to make a hole in the bottom of the cup, fill the cup with soil, and plant one or two dried lima or kidney beans near the panel. Place on a tray and keep the soil moist. To view their seeds, students remove the rubber band and pull down the panel.

Encourage children to make daily observations of their seeds and to note changes. Have them start a plant diary in which they pretend to be their sprouting seed. Ask children to make daily entries describing what is happening to the seed and how it feels about these changes. Ask for volunteers to share their entries. Are the seeds growing at different rates? Discuss how plants are similar to people in that they all grow at their own pace!

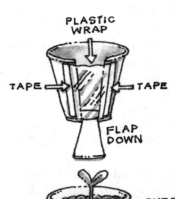

PLASTIC WRAP

TAPE ← → TAPE

FLAP DOWN

RUBBER BAND

Sunflowers

MAKE SUNFLOWER MASKS

To enhance children's play-reading experience, let students don sunflower face masks. Provide children with large yellow paper plates and help them cut out eye and mouth holes. Then hand out unshelled sunflower seeds, glue, and yellow and orange paper. Invite students to glue seeds around the center of the plate, and to glue cutout paper petals around the plate's rim. Show them how

to tie the masks on with string. For more fun, invite students to make "bees" out of cotton balls and construction paper scraps. Students can cut out tiny features and glue them onto the cotton balls to make bee faces and antennae. Invite the "sunflowers" to wear their masks during readings of the play, while the "bees" go visiting from flower to flower.

Me and My Shadow

SHADOW PUPPET PLAYS

After reading the play, discuss ways shadows look different from the objects that make them. (A shadow is flat and shows the outline of an object, but not its features.) Then let children explore the science behind shadows as they produce plays with shadow puppet performers. Have children make simple puppets out of cardboard. They can poke holes for eyes or use scissors to snip out other features, then tape the puppets to rulers or unsharpened pencils. Make a simple stage by cutting an opening in a large box and taping pieces of waxed paper across the opening to make a screen. Darken the room and shine a lamp behind the screen. Have students hold their puppets between the light and the screen. Suggest that they move their puppets closer to and farther from the light to explore different effects.

Stormy Weather

STORM SOUNDS

Ask children to name different kinds of weather and list these on a chart. (rain, hail, wind, thunder) Go down the list, asking, "What different sounds do you hear during each kind of weather?" Record responses. Then, divide the class into groups—one group for each kind of weather on the list. Invite the groups to take turns presenting sounds for their weather type. Encourage children to notice not only the kind of sound being made, but also the way the sounds are made. For example, you can ask the observers, "Were the wind group's sounds quiet or loud? Why do you think this group made the wind sound that way?"

Neighbors in Space

PICK A PLANET

Ask students to choose one of the planets or the sun and invite them to learn more about it. Children can look at picture books or consult a librarian for help with their research. After they have learned new facts about their planet or the sun, change the play to include the new information. Read the play as a class so that everyone can learn the newfound facts.

All About Animals

Get Set for a Pet

PET POLLS AND GRAPHS

Take a pet poll in your class. Begin by asking, "Do you have a pet?" and help children make a simple bar graph, with a Yes and a No column, to record their responses. Help students interpret their data by asking, "Which column has the most names in it?" "How many children in our class have pets? How many do not?" Then take additional polls and make more graphs by inviting children to pose other pet questions, such as, "What Kinds of Pets Do You Have?" "How Many Pets Do You Have?" or "What Pet Do You Wish You Had?" Ask questions such as, "Do more children in our class have dogs or fish?" "How many pets do we have altogether?" "Which pet do most children wish they had? How do you know?"

Guinea Pig Song

CLOSE-UP ON PETS

This play is about children observing their classroom pet. Is there a pet in your classroom? If so, help students hone their observation skills and express their observations through speaking or writing. Invite your class to observe the pet closely. Encourage them to notice how and what the pet eats. Have they seen the pet sleep? Does the pet play? What does it like to do? If there is not a pet in your classroom, ask children to imagine one that they might like to have. The pet can be a real animal or a make-believe one. Instead of observing an actual animal, children can do research by reading simple books, looking at pictures, or using their imagination to identify a make-believe pet's characteristics and habits.

New Frog in the Pond

FURTHER FROG POND ADVENTURES

Ask children to imagine what might happen with the frogs after the play ends. What other things might the frogs do together? What kinds of adventures might they have? Use children's responses to add another scene or several scenes to the play. After reading your new frog play together, ask, "What things might you do to help someone new to your neighborhood feel welcome?" Use this information to write a new play together about a child who is new to their neighborhood.

A Duckling Tale

ALL IN A LIFE CYCLE

As a class, research the life cycle of a duck from egg to adult. Then make a class circle-shaped mural depicting each stage in the process. Afterward, ask, "What other animal's life cycle would you like to find out about?" Record children's responses, then divide the class into groups based on their choices. Help each group research their animal and make a circle-shaped mural about it. Display the murals and help students compare them. Ask: "How is a [dog's] life cycle different from that of a duck? How is it the same?" Depending on the types of animals chosen, this can be an opportunity to discuss the differences among mammals, birds, amphibians, reptiles, and fish.

Fish School

RULES TO LIVE BY

After reading the play, see if your class can come up with other rules the fish school may have. Use this discussion as a springboard to ask children to come up with their own set of class rules. What are some things the class can do to keep themselves orderly? Some examples may include: talking out problems, not hitting, raising your hand to speak, etc. Invite children to work in teams to write and illustrate their ideas on tagboard or sturdy paper. Then join the pictures to make a banner and display it in a prominent place in the classroom so that it can be referred to all year long.

Ready to Fly

COMINGS AND GOINGS

Explain to students that some animals migrate—move from place to place—to find better weather and more food. Most travel to warmer places in winter and then return to their original habitat in the spring. Pick a bird in your region that migrates and consult a field guide to birds to find out about its migratory route and destination. Plot the bird's migration route on a map. Then, learn about other migrating birds and plot their courses as well. One unique bird to learn about is the arctic tern. This bird migrates from the North Pole to the South Pole and back, flying halfway around the world twice a year! To take your class's migration studies further, help students find out about other migrating animals, including ladybugs, bats, salmon, caribou, and butterflies.

D Is for Dinosaur

GOING ON A DIG

Explain to students that scientists called archaeologists dig for dinosaur bones and other relics of the past. Create your own dig site and invite your class to become amateur archaeologists. Fill large boxes or dishpans with dirt or sand. Bury everyday objects in the boxes (buttons; shells; rocks; clean, cooked chicken bones; paper clips) without letting the children know what you've buried. Let students use plastic spoons and old paintbrushes to dig up and dust off the objects, and then have them write stories about the items they found. Tell them to pretend that they've never seen these things before. Encourage them to create a history around the object and give it a new name based on its characteristics or possible uses.

PLAYS FOR ANYTIME

Pop! Pop! Popcorn!

POPCORN PANTOMIMES

Give your students an opportunity to listen to popcorn popping—and munch it! You can either use a popcorn popper or pop it the old-fashioned way—by heating it in oil in a pan on the stove. Invite students to describe what they hear (at first, there are just a few pops; the popping then builds as the kernels pop more rapidly, and then the popping sounds peter out as fewer and fewer kernels are left). Then, invite students to pretend they are kernels of popcorn popping, starting out with a pop now and then, then getting more and more frequent, and gradually popping less and less. Have students take turns playing the *pip!* kernel. When the *pip!* kernel pops up, have that child choose a different movement from the rest of the class to distinguish that kernel from the others.

Big, Bad Cold

BE WELL, STAY WELL

After reading the play together, encourage your class to contribute pages to a "How We Stay Healthy" big book to keep in your classroom all year. Ask students to suggest things they can do, not only to prevent a cold, but to stay healthy in general. Some suggestions may include: wash your hands often; cover your mouth and nose when sneezing or coughing; exercise; eat plenty of fruits and vegetables, etc. Then, have students write and illustrate their ideas and bind the pages together with "O" rings.

Loose Tooth

TOOTH TALES

Create a chart on classroom tooth loss. List all of the children's names on the chart. Then write how many teeth, if any, each child has lost. As students lose teeth throughout the year, invite them to update the chart. If possible, take a photograph of each child as he or she loses a tooth. Hang the photos near the chart. Then take a photograph after the child's new tooth has grown in. Place it next to the lost-tooth photo. Invite children to share tooth-loss stories and what rituals, if any, take place in their family when they lose a tooth. If you can remember a story of your own, share it with your class.

Time for the Party!

STORYBOOK BIRTHDAY

Choose a favorite character from a book your class has read together. Then plan a birthday party for that character. Ask children to consider what they would need for the party. Who should be invited? What kinds of presents or decorations would the character like? Then set a time to have the party. Set the book on a chair in place of the character or invite students to draw pictures of the character and display these on a bulletin board. Let children make cards and presents for the character, or draw pictures of the kinds of presents they would bring. Serve food, choosing treats the class is sure the character would like!

The Name Game

GETTING TO KNOW YOU

This play can come in handy as a name-learning game for the beginning of the school year to help children (and you!) learn one another's names. After children have read the play using their own names, invite them to pair up and insert their partner's name in the play instead. For example, "Her name is _____. That rhymes with _____." (Tell children that they can make up words that rhyme.) Then have the other partner do the same with the first child's name. Continue switching partners until everyone has had a chance to learn each student's name. You may wish to take part in the game, also, to make it extra fun for the class and as an aid in learning the names of your students. (This play is also a great activity to perform on Visitors' Day—invite parents, guardians, and other visitors to participate with children.)

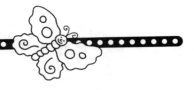

We Go to School

WALK OR RIDE?

Before reading this play, take a survey to find out how children in your class get to school. If there are students in each group depicted in the play, have them read that part. If not, let students choose whichever part they like. Later, create a human graph that shows the way students get to school. Have students stand or sit behind one another in rows. (One row consists of walkers, another bus riders, etc.) Ask volunteers to draw a picture to represent each group. Then invite students to step out of their row, one by one, and observe the graph (while you take that student's place in the row). Ask questions, such as, "How do most of the children in our class get to school?" "How do the fewest children get to school?" "How many children take the bus?" and so on.

We Are Your Community

WHO AM I?

Let students brush up their acting skills with this entertaining pantomime activity. First ask them to name the community helpers mentioned in the play. List these on the board. Then ask them to come up with others to add to the list. (store clerk, dentist, newspaper carrier, sanitation worker, druggist, nurse, pizza maker, etc.) Have students then take turns acting out one of these roles while classmates try to guess their identities.

The Magic Place

LOOK FOR A BOOK

Plan a field trip to your local library. Ask a librarian to give your class a tour, so that children learn where to look for favorite books when they visit. If some of your students don't have library cards, take this opportunity to get cards for them. Tell them that their library card is their ticket to the magic place they read about in the play.

Llegó el otoño

Personajes

Hoja 1   Hoja 2

Hoja 1: ¿Estás lista?

Hoja 2: No, no estoy lista.

Hoja 1: ¿Por qué no?

Hoja 2: Tengo miedo.

Hoja 1: No tengas miedo.
¡Ven, es muy divertido!

Hoja 2: ¿Cómo lo sabes?

Hoja 1: Porque sí.

Hoja 2: Yo no estoy segura.

Hoja 1: ¡Vamos! Prueba.

Hoja 2: Bueno, está bien.

Hoja 1:   ¡Preparada!

Hoja 2:   ¡Lista!

Las dos juntas: ¡Ya!

Hoja 1:   ¡Yupiii! ¡Qué divertido!

Hoja 2:   ¡Yupiii! ¡Es verdad!

Hoja 1:   Voy cayendo suavemente.

Hoja 2:   Voy volando por el aire.

Hoja 1:   ¿Lista para aterrizar?

Hoja 2:   Sí, estoy lista.

Hoja 1:   Vamos.

Hoja 2:   ¡Qué bien que aterrizamos!

Hoja 1:   Me cansé.

Hoja 2:   Yo también.

Hoja 1:   Es hora de descansar.

Hoja 2:   ¡Que duermas bien!

Fin

Ruidos otoñales

Personajes

Pisahoja 1	Pisahoja 3	Pisahoja 5
Pisahoja 2	Pisahoja 4	Pisahoja 6

Pisahoja 1: ¡Chis! ¡Chas!
¿Qué es ese ruidito?

Pisahoja 2: ¡Chis! ¡Chas!
¿Es un pajarito?

Pisahoja 3: ¡Chis! ¡Chas!
Escucha ese ruidito.

Pisahoja 4: ¡Chis! ¡Chas!
¿Es un ratoncito?

Pisahoja 5: ¡Chis! ¡Chas!
¿Es un arroyo?

Pisahoja 6: ¡Chis! ¡Chas!
¡No, son hojas de otoño!

Fin

Copos de nieve

Personajes

Copo de nieve 1	Copo de nieve 3	Copo de nieve 5
Copo de nieve 2	Copo de nieve 4	Copo de nieve 6

Copo de nieve 1: Soy un copo de nieve.
Me parezco a una flor.

Copo de nieve 2: Soy un copo de nieve.
Me parezco a una estrella.

Copo de nieve 3: Soy un copo de nieve.
Me parezco a un diamante.

·················➤

25 Spanish Plays for Emergent Readers　Scholastic Professional Books

Copo de nieve 4:   Soy un copo de nieve.
                                          Me parezco a una nube.

Copo de nieve 5:   Soy un copo de nieve.
                                          Me parezco a un caramelo.

Copo de nieve 6:   Soy un copo de nieve.
                                          Me parezco a una rueda.

Todos juntos: Somos todos diferentes,
                                     pero todos somos copos de nieve.
                                     Y todos juntos,
                                     ¡hacemos un muñeco de nieve!

Fin

Día de la marmota

Personajes

Marmota 1   Marmota 2

Marmota 1: ¡Hmm! ¡Qué siesta tan buena y tan larga!

Marmota 2: Tienes razón. ¡Me siento muy bien!

Marmota 1: Creo que debemos levantarnos.

Marmota 2: Sí, ya es hora.

Marmota 1: ¡Primero me despereezzzzo!

Marmota 2: Yo también me desperezzzzo. ¡Qué rico se siente!

Marmota 1: Bueno, ya estoy lista. Voy a salir. ┄┄┄┄┄┄→

Marmota 2:   Esperaré aquí.

Marmota 1:   Recuerda, si veo mi sombra,
tendremos otras seis semanas de invierno.

Marmota 2:   Y si no la ves . . .

Las dos juntas: ¡Pronto será primavera!

Marmota 1:   Hasta pronto.

Marmota 2:   ¡Buena suerte!

Marmota 1:   Por el agujero voy. Veo una luz.
Ya estoy casi afuera. ¡Eh! Estoy afuera.*

* Para terminar la obra, lee el final 1 o el final 2   ....➤

Final 1

Marmota 1: ¡Ahí está mi sombra!
Debo decirle a mi amiga.
Entro en la cuevita.
¡Eh amiga! ¡Vuelve a la cama!

Marmota 2: Bueno. Hasta dentro de seis
semanas. ¡Buenas noches!

Fin

Final 2

Marmota 1: ¿Dónde está mi sombra?
¡No la veo! Debo decirle a mi amiga.
Entro en la cuevita.
¡Eh, es hora de levantarse!

Marmota 2: ¡Vamos, viene la Primavera!

Fin

¡Viva la primavera!

Personajes

Amigos de la primavera 1, 2, 3, 4, 5, 6, 7, 8, 9, 10, 11, y 12

Amigo 1:	En invierno llueve y nieva.
Amigo 2:	Y ni una flor nos queda.
Amigo 3:	¡Cantemos y bailemos!
Amigos 1, 2, y 3:	Que llega la primavera.
Amigo 4:	Los pajaritos cantan.
Amigo 5:	Y las bellas mariposas,
Amigo 6:	sobre las flores se posan.
Amigos 4, 5, y 6:	¡Ya llegó la primavera

Amigo 7:   El cielo se llena de sol.

Amigo 8:   Las flores se pintan de color.

Amigo 9:   El aire es fresco y perfumado.

**Amigos
7, 8, y 9:**   ¡Aquí está la primavera!

Amigo 10:   Y pronto llega el verano.

Amigo 11:   Y el otoño viene en un tris,

Amigo 12:   pero, por el momento

**Amigos
10, 11, y 12:**   ¡La primavera nos hace feliz!

Todos: ¡Viva la primavera!

Fin

De la semilla a la planta

Personajes

Semilla/Planta	Agua
Suelo	Sol

Semilla: Soy una semillita.
Un día quiero ser
una planta verde y grande,
¡que todos podrán ver!

Suelo: Soy el suelo y a la semilla doy
un hogar cómodo para crecer.
Le doy calor y protección,
cuando sopla el viento frío de la estación.

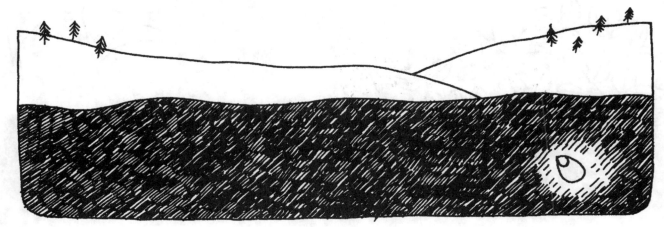

Agua: Soy el agua y a la semilla daré

mis gotitas para beber.

Luego, la semilla crecerá,

¡mucho antes de que la puedas ver!

Sol: Soy el Sol y con mis fuertes rayos

brillaré sobre la semilla.

Le daré calor y luz brillante,

dos cosas que necesita para ser grande.

Planta: ¡Oh! ¡Miren! Ya soy una planta.

Todos ustedes me ayudaron.

Cada uno a su manera es especial,

pero juntos me han hecho germinar.

Fin

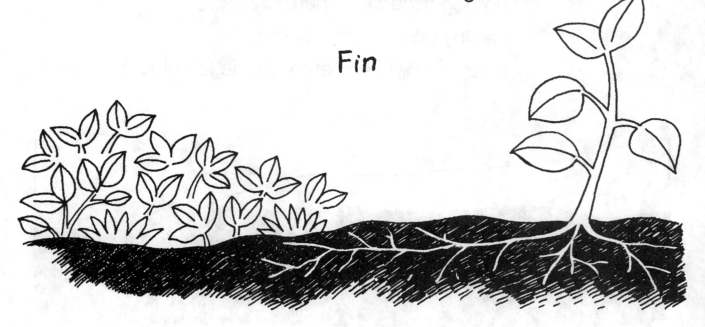

25 Spanish Plays for Emergent Readers   Scholastic Professional Books

Girasoles

Personajes

Grupo de Girasoles 1   Grupo de Girasoles 2

Grupo de Girasoles 1:   Somos girasoles.

Grupo de Girasoles 2:   Nos parecemos al Sol.

Grupo de Girasoles 1:   Nuestras flores son grandes.

Grupo de Girasoles 2:   Amarillo es nuestro color.

Grupo de Girasoles 1:   En el campo florecemos.

Grupo de Girasoles 2:   Con el viento juguetón.

Grupo de Girasoles 1:   Siempre crecemos muy alto.

Grupo de Girasoles 2:   Siempre miramos al Sol.

Grupo de Girasoles 1:   Las abejas nos visitan.

Grupo de Girasoles 2:   Sobre todo al mediodía.

Grupo de Girasoles 1:   Los pájaros también.

Grupo de Girasoles 2:   Nos tienen compañía.

Grupo de Girasoles 1:   ¡Nunca estamos solos!
¡Tenemos muchos amigos!

Grupo de Girasoles 2:   ¡Cuánto nos divertimos!

Fin

Mi sombra y yo

Personajes

Niño   Sombra

Niño: ¿Quién eres tú?

Sombra: Yo soy tú.

Niño: ¿Qué cosas haces?

Sombra: Lo que haces tú.

Niño: Si voy para adelante.

Sombra: Voy adelante también.

................▶

Niño:	Si voy para atrás.
Sombra:	Voy para atrás también.
Niño:	Si doy un salto.
Sombra:	Doy un salto también.
Niño:	Si corro, corro, corro.
Sombra:	Yo corro también.
Niño:	Creo que eres un amigo especial.
Sombra:	Siempre estaremos juntos.
Niño:	Nunca estaré solo, porque te tengo a ti.
Sombra:	¡Yo también porque te tengo a ti!

Fin

25 Spanish Plays for Emergent Readers Scholastic Professional Books

Tiempo de tormenta

Personajes

Lluvia 1	Viento
Lluvia 2	Rayo
Lluvia 3	Trueno

Lluvia 1:   ¡Plic!

Lluvia 2:   ¡Ploc!

Lluvia 3:   ¡Plic! ¡Ploc!

Lluvia 1:   ¡Plic!

Lluvia 2:   ¡Ploc!

Lluvia 3:   ¡Plic, Ploc!

Viento: ¡Shhhh!

Rayo: ¡Crack! ·················>

Trueno:	Retumba, truena.
Viento:	¡Shhhh!
Rayo:	¡Crack!
Trueno:	Retumba, truena.
Lluvia 1:	Llovizna, llovizna.
Lluvia 2:	Llovizna, llovizna.
Lluvia 3:	Llovizna, llovizna.
Viento:	¡Shuusshhh! ¡Shuusshhh!
Rayo:	¡Crrr-rack! ¡Crack!
Trueno:	Retumba, truena. ¡Bum, bum, bum!
Lluvia 1:	Plin, plan. Plin, plan, plon.
Lluvia 2:	Plin, plan. Plin, plan, plon.
Lluvia 3:	Plin, plan. Plin, plan, plon.
Viento:	¡Shuusshhh! ¡Vuusshhh!

Rayo: ¡Crack!

Trueno: Retumba, truena.

Lluvia 1: Llovizna, llovizna.

Lluvia 2: Llovizna, llovizna.

Lluvia 3: Llovizna, llovizna.

Lluvia 1: ¡Plic! ¡Ploc!

Lluvia 2: ¡Plic!

Lluvia 3: ¡Ploc!

Viento: Shhhh!

Lluvia 1: ¡Plic! ¡Ploc!

Lluvia 2: ¡Plic!

Lluvia 3: ¡Ploc!

Fin

Vecinos en el espacio

Personajes

Sol

Los planetas:	Mercurio	Marte	Urano
	Venus	Júpiter	Neptuno
	Tierra	Saturno	Plutón

Los planetas: Somos los planetas.

Sol: Yo soy el Sol.

Los planetas: Somos los planetas.

Sol: Yo soy el Sol.

Todos juntos: ¡Somos vecinos en el espacio!

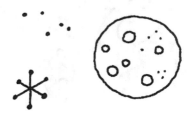

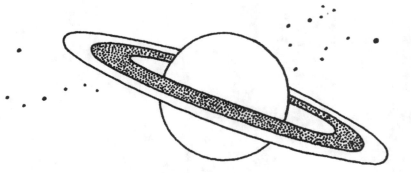

Sol: Yo soy el Sol.
ℹSoy la estrella más brillante del cielo!
Todos los planetas se mueven a mi alrededor.

Mercurio: Yo soy Mercurio.
Vivo al lado del Sol.
El Sol me mantiene calentito.

Venus: Yo soy Venus.
ℹMe llaman "Lucero de la tarde"
porque tan brillante soy!

Tierra: Sí, tú brillas, pero yo soy
la Tierra, ℹel único planeta lleno de vida!

Marte: Quizás, pero no eres de color rojo
brillante como yo. ℹYo soy Marte!

Júpiter: Y que dirán de mí. Soy el gran Júpiter.
ℹEl más grande planeta de todos!

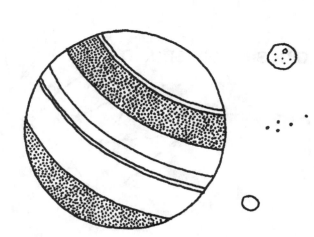

Saturno: Yo soy Saturno, la joya más hermosa del sistema solar. ¡Admiren mis anillos!

Urano: Yo soy Urano. Giro de costado. Por eso soy diferente y especial.

Neptuno: Yo soy Neptuno. Nunca estoy solo. ¡Mi pequeño amigo Plúton está a mi lado todo el tiempo!

Plutón: Soy el planeta más pequeño, pero también el más frío. Soy Plutón. ¡Brrrrrr!

Los planetas: Somos los planetas.

Sol: Yo soy el Sol.

Los planetas: Somos los planetas.

Sol: Yo soy el Sol.

Todos juntos: ¡Somos vecinos en el espacio!

Fin

Si quieres una mascota...

Personajes

Pez   Pájaro   Gato   Perro

Todos juntos: Somos las mascotas,
y venimos a decirles
que si nos quieren adoptar,
nos tienen que cuidar
de manera muy especial.

Pececito: Yo soy un pececito.
Necesito un acuario limpio, agua fresca,
comida para peces y mucho, mucho amor.

Pajarito: Yo soy un pajarito.
              Necesito una jaula limpia, agua fresca,
              comida para pájaros y mucho, mucho amor.

Gato: Yo soy un gato.
              Necesito una cama suave, agua fresca,
              comida para gatos, y mucho amor.

Perro: Yo soy un perro.
              Necesito una cama suave, agua fresca,
              comida para perros, largos paseos, caricias
              y mucho amor.

Todos juntos: Si quieren una mascota,
              recuerden lo que decimos:
              Necesitamos mucho amor
              y todos los días, mucho mimo.

Fin

Canción del Conejillo de Indias

Personajes

Conejillos de Indias   1, 2, 3, 4, 5, 6, 7, 8, 9, 10, 11, 12, and 13

Conejillo de Indias 1:   Conejillo de Indias, sentado en mi regazo.

Conejillo de Indias 2:   Conejillo de Indias, te doy un abrazo.

Conejillo de Indias 3:   Conejillo de Indias, entra en tu jaulita.

Conejillo de Indias 4:   Conejillo de Indias, ¡rápido!, que te la quitan.

Conejillo de Indias 5:   Conejillo de Indias, ¿cómo te llamas?

Conejillo de Indias 6:   Conejillo de Indias,
corre por la casa.

Conejillo de Indias 7:   Conejillo de Indias,
¿quieres irte a la cama?

Conejillo de Indias 8:   Conejillo de Indias,
duerme la siesta.

Conejillo de Indias 9:   Conejillo de Indias,
primero ven a comer.

Conejillo de Indias 10:   Conejillo de Indias,
¡Crunch! ¡Crunch! ¡Crunch!

Conejillo de Indias 11:   Conejillo de Indias,
¿qué dices?

Conejillo de Indias 12:   Conejillo de Indias,
¡Cuic! ¡Cuic!

Conejillo de Indias 13:   Conejillo de Indias,
¿sabes una cosa?

Todos juntos: Conejillo de Indias,
¡te queremos mucho!

Fin

Las ranitas saltarinas

Personajes

Rana 1   Rana 2

Rana 1:   ¿Quién eres?

Rana 2:   Soy una rana.

Rana 1:   Yo también.
¿eres nueva por aquí?

Rana 2:   Sí, soy nueva aquí.

Rana 1:   ¿Te gusta este charco?

Rana 2:   Si, me gusta mucho
este charco.

Rana 1:   ¿Puedes saltar?

Rana 2:   Sí, puedo saltar.

Rana 1:   Muéstrame como saltas.

Rana 2:   ¡Arriba! ¡Arriba!

Rana 1:   ¡Qué bien que saltas!

Rana 2:   Gracias.

Rana 1:   ¿Quieres ser mi amiga?

Rana 2:   Sí, me gustaría mucho.

Rana 1:   Ven, vamos a saltar.

Rana 2:   Sí, saltemos.

Fin

Un cuento para patito

Personajes

Patito   Mamá pata

Patito: Mami, cuéntame un cuento.

Mamá Pata: Sí, mi patito.
¿Qué cuento quieres que te cuente?

Patito: Cuéntame de cuando nací.

Mamá Pata: Bueno. Estabas dentro de un
huevo pequeño y blanco.
Me senté encima del huevo
para mantenerlo calentito.

Patito: ¿Y cómo hacía para comer?

Mamá Pata: Dentro del huevo había toda la comida que necesitabas.

Patito: Y entonces, ¿qué pasó?

Mamá Pata: Un día, rompiste el cascarón del huevo con tu piquito.

Patito: ¡Ya estaba listo para salir!

Mamá Pata: Sí. Picoteaste y picoteaste el cascarón. Así fue cómo saliste del huevo.

Patito: ¿Qué pasó después?

Mamá Pata: ¡Fuiste mi lindo patito lleno de plumas!

Patito: ¿Mami?

Mamá Pata: ¿Sí, mi patito?

Patito: Estoy contento de haber nacido.

Mamá Pata: Yo también, mi patito querido.

Fin

Escuela de pececitos

Personajes

Srta. Pez	Alumno pez 1	Alumno pez 3
	Alumno pez 2	Alumno pez 4

Srta. Pez: ¡Buenos días, clase!

Todos los pececitos: ¡Buenos días, señorita Pez!

Srta. Pez: Hoy estudiaremos las reglas de nuestra escuelita de peces. ¿Qué deben hacer si quieren decir algo?

Alumno Pez 1: ¡Levantar nuestras aletas!

Srta. Pez:	¡Muy bien! ¿Cómo hay que sentarse en los asientos?
Alumno Pez 2:	Con nuestras colas sobre el piso.
Srta. Pez:	¡Muy bien! ¿Qué pasa si traen lombrices para el almuerzo?
Alumno Pez 3:	Hay que traer bastante para compartir con los otros.
Srta. Pez:	Sí. ¿Y si alguien te hace enojar?
Alumno Pez 4:	Debemos hablar antes y no enojarnos ¡Y no soplar burbujas en la cara de los otros!
Srta. Pez:	¡Excelente trabajo! Ahora, ¿qué quieren aprender hoy?
Todos los pececitos:	¡Sobre la gente!

Fin

Listos para volar

Personajes

Pájaro 1   Pájaro 2   Pájaro 3   Pájaro 4

Pájaro 1: ¡Brrrr! ¡Se está poniendo frío aquí en el norte! Ya es hora de irnos.

Pájaro 2: ¿Hora de irnos adónde?

Pájaro 3: ¡Al sur, tontita! Eso es lo que los pájaros hacen.

Pájaro 4: Cuando aquí comienza a hacer frío, volamos hacia de sur donde está calentito.

Pájaro 2: ¿Qué debo llevar?

Pájaro 1: Nada. ¡Pero, debes prepararte a comer muchas lombrices!

Pájaro 2: ¡Lombrices! ¡Humm, que rico! Pero, ¿por qué debemos volar al sur para comer lombrices?

Pájaro 3: Las lombrices se mueren cuando hace frío. Pero en el sur hay muchas lombrices, porque hace calor.

Pájaro 2: ¡Qué bueno! Nos podemos quedar allí siempre.

Pájaro 4: No. Dentro de unos meses hará frío en el sur.

Pájaro 1: Y hará calor aquí en el norte.

Pájaro 2: Entonces ¿volaremos de vuelta aquí? ¿Qué pasará con las lombrices?

Pájaro 3: Cuando aquí el tiempo se ponga caliente de nuevo habrá muchas lombrices.

Pájaro 2: Ahora entiendo. Tiempo caliente y lombrices. No esperemos más. ¡Vamos!

Fin

Con D de dinosaurio

Personajes

Tanya   Sam   Ruby

Tanya: Dinosaurio se escribe con D.

Sam: Dinosaurio se escribe con D.

Ruby: Dinosaurio se escribe con D.

Todos: ¡Sí, así es!

Tanya: ¿Has visto alguna vez un dinosaurio?

Sam: No. Nunca vi un dinosaurio.
                No se puede ver a los dinosaurios.
                Ya no existen más.

Ruby: Yo vi un dinosaurio.

Tanya: No, no lo has visto.

Ruby: Sí, lo vi. Ayer vi un
                dinosaurio.

· · · · · · · · ·>

Sam: ¿Dónde lo viste?

Ruby: Fui al museo.
Allí lo vi.
Es un dinosaurio grande y huesudo.
¡Y se llama Tiranosaurus Rex!

Tanya y Sam: ¡Oh!

Ruby: ¿Quieren ver al dinosaurio?

Tanya: ¡Sí, quiero verlo!

Sam: Vamos a ver al dinosaurio.

Todos: ¡Vamos!

Tanya: Dinosaurio se escribe con D.

Sam: Dinosaurio se escribe con D.

Ruby: Dinosaurio se escribe con D.

Todos: Sí, así es.

Fin

Palomitas

Personajes

Palomita 1, 2, 3, 4, 5, 6, y 7

Palomita 1:   ¡Plop!

Palomita 2:   ¡Plop!

Palomita 3:   ¡Plop! ¡Plop!

Palomita 4:   ¡Plop! ¡Plop!

Palomita 5:   ¡Plop! ¡Plop! ¡Plop!

Palomita 6:   ¡Plop! ¡Plop! ¡Plop!

Palomita 7:   ¡Plip!

**Palomitas
1 a 6:**   ¿Plip?

Palomita 7:   ¡Plop!

Fin

¡Un resfrío muy fuerte!

Personajes

Nariz tapada	Tos	Fiebre
Estornudo	Dolor de garganta	

Nariz tapada: Soy la nariz tapada.
¡Sniff! ¡Sniff! ¡Sniff!

Estornudo: Soy el estornudo.
¡Atchis! ¡Atchis! ¡Atchis!

Tos: Soy la tos.
¡Cof! ¡Cof! ¡Cof!

Dolor de garganta: Soy el dolor de garganta.
¡Ay! ¡Ay! ¡Ay!

Fiebre: Soy la fiebre.
¡Caliente! ¡Caliente!

Todos juntos: Y cuando juntamos todo eso, ¿qué somos?
¡Un resfrío muy fuerte!

Fin

El diente flojo

Nick: ¡Hola amigos! ¡Miren lo que traigo! Mi mamá me dio unas ricas manzanas rojas.

Mi Won: ¡Manzanas! ¡Qué rico!

Jerome: ¿Me das una?

Raj: ¿A mí también?

Nick: Sí, hay manzanas para todos.

Ana:　　Yo no puedo comer manzanas.

Mi Won:　　¿Por qué no?

Ana:　　Tengo un diente flojo.

Nick:　　¿Un diente flojo? ¡Qué suerte!

Ana:　　¿Qué suerte?

Jerome:　　Quiere decir que estás creciendo.

Ana:　　¡Sí! ¡Qué bien!

Raj:　　Dentro de poco tu diente
se caerá.

Nick:　　Y uno nuevo más grande,
te saldrá en el mismo lugar.

Ana:　　Entonces, podré comer todas
las manzanas que me dé la gana.
¡Tengan cuidado, manzanas!

Fin

¡Viva la fiesta!

Personajes

Cumpleañero	Pastel	Helado	Amigos
Globos	Velitas	Regalos	

Cumpleañero: Hoy es mi cumpleaños.
¡Tengo todo lo que necesito
para una gran fiesta!

Globos: Somos los globos.
¡Alegres y de todos
los colores!

Pastel: Yo soy el pastel.
¡Estoy cubierto de azúcar!

Velitas: Nosotros somos las velitas.
Si nos cuentas sabrás cuánto
cumples. ·············▶

Helado: Soy el helado.
Soy frío y sabroso!

Regalos: Somos los regalos.
¡Qué sorpresa te llevarás!

Cumpleañero: ¡A festejar!
¡Un momento! ¡Falta algo!

Globos: Hay globos.

Pastel: Hay pastel.

Velitas: Hay velitas.

Helado: Hay helado.

Regalos: Hay regalos.

Cumpleañero: ¿Qué falta?

Amigos: ¡Los amigos!

Todos: ¡Ahora sí, a festejar!

Fin

El juego del nombre

Todos juntos: Yo me llamo . . .

Tú te llamas . . .

A todos nos gusta jugar

al juego de nombrar.

Jugador 1:   Me llamo _____.

Mi nombre rima con _____.

Jugador 2:   Me llamo _____.

Mi nombre rima con _____.

Marcelo

Miguel

Rosana

Jugador 3:   Me llamo _____.

Mi nombre rima con _____.

Jugador 4:   Me llamo _____.

Mi nombre rima con _____.

Jugador 5:   Me llamo _____.

Mi nombre rima con _____.

(El juego continua hasta que todos los jugadores hayan jugado.)

Todos juntos: Estos son nuestros nombres.
Como ves, no hay dos iguales.
Esperamos que con este juego
te hayas divertido en grande.

Fin

Vamos a la escuela

Personajes

Grupo en autobús   Grupo en auto
Grupo en bicicleta   Grupo a pie

Grupo en autobus: Vamos en autobús,
en autobús,
en autobús,
Así vamos a la escuela.
Vamos en autobús.

Grupo en bicicleta: Vamos en bicicleta,
en bicicleta,
en bicicleta,
Así vamos a la escuela.
Vamos en bicicleta.

Grupo en auto: Vamos en auto,
en auto,
en auto,
Así vamos a la escuela.
Vamos en auto.

Grupo a pie: Vamos a pie,
a pie,
a pie,
Así vamos a la escuela.
Vamos a pie.

Todos juntos: De cualquier manera que sea,
vamos a la escuela,
vamos a la escuela.
De cualquier manera que sea
Nos gusta ir a la escuela.!

Fin

25 Spanish Plays for Emergent Readers Scholastic Professional Books

Somos tu comunidad

Personajes

| Niño | Bombero | Bibliotecaria | Amigos |
| Policía | Maestro | Cartero | |

Niño: Me acabo de mudar a este lugar.
              ¿Quién más vive aquí?

Todos los otros: La comunidad, la comunidad.
                        Somos la comunidad.
                        La comunidad, la comunidad.
                        Haremos que te guste vivir aquí.

Policía: Yo soy el policía.
                 Te daré seguridad.   ················➤

Bombero: Yo soy el bombero.
Apagaré los inciendos.

Maestra: Yo soy la maestra.
Te enseñaré cosas nuevas.

Bibliotecaria: Yo soy la bibliotecaria.
Te ayudaré a encontrar buenos
libros para leer.

Cartero: Yo soy el cartero.
Te traeré tus cartas.

Amigos: Nosotros somos los amigos.
Te daremos la bienvenida.

Niño: ¡Oh! Creo que me gustará vivir aquí.
Estoy contento de vivir en esta comunidad.

Fin

25 Spanish Plays for Emergent Readers Scholastic Professional Books

El lugar mágico

Personajes

Luke	María	Tamika	Seth

Luke: ¡Eh! ¿adónde van?

María: Vamos a un lugar mágico.

Luke: ¿Qué clase de lugar mágico?

Tamika: Un lugar que nos lleve a todos lados y nos muestre de todo.

Luke: ¿Qué quieren decir?

Seth: Que podamos visitar China o África.

María: Dónde podamos ver a George Washington
o a la Cenicienta.

Tamika: ¿Quieres venir con nosotros?

Luke: No sé. Me da miedo.

Seth: No tengas miedo.
¡Es un lugar fantástico!

Luke: Bueno, está bien. Vamos.

María: Ya llegamos.

Luke: ¡Es la biblioteca!

Tamika: Sí. Es un lugar mágico.

Seth: Con todos estos libros,
podemos viajar a cualquier lado.

Luke: ¿Qué estamos esperando?
¡Entremos!

Fin